HOPE FOR THE HELPFUL

Sometimes The Picker-Uppers Need A "Pick Me Up"

By

JOHN ALSTON

Table of Contents

INTRODUCTION

Not all Heroes wear Capes

You are the one who runs into the face of danger, the one that everyone calls for when there is trouble, the one who rushes to car wrecks at 1 am, the one who pulls people out of fires and accidents – the one who rescues people from all sorts of horrible situations. You are the one who gives people hope and encouragement but who's got your back? Who takes care of your raging emotions? Who helps relieve your stress? How do you survive living in a constant rush of adrenaline and cortisol?

No one sees the struggles going on inside or notices the pain that you constantly try to hide. The truth is that you don't have to hide your pain and the problems you are going through. Sometimes, heroes need help as well and this book is dedicated to helping you come out of the emotional mess that

1

accumulates as a result of everything you have to go through in your job and life.

A lot of first responders such as firefighters, paramedics, Emergency Medical Technicians (EMT), police officers and active duty military personnel all have to deal with unimaginable psychological and emotional problems and this is directly due to the nature of their jobs.

Firefighters and first responders face a lot of personal issues ranging from depression, stress and post-traumatic stress disorders, suicidal thoughts, substance abuse, and addiction. I know. I've been there. After more than 34 years of responding to all types of emergencies, I have worked with some incredible people. I lost two fire fighter friends to suicide. There have been a few others who have attempted it, as well. Your pain is real, but you don't have to face it alone.

We need to view emotional and psychological injuries the way we view any other injury our members face in the performance of their duties.

A survey conducted by the American Psychological Association consistently finds that your job is a major source of stress. I acknowledge that you may not avoid the situations that create these tensions, but in subsequent chapters, you may learn how you can take steps to manage work-related stress.

The examples used in this work are not attributable to any one person or a specific incident. They are a hybrid of real incidents to give the reader an idea of what first responders face.

"Dum Spiro Spero"...While I Breathe I Hope.

CHAPTER 1

A lot more than "the Blues"

Bart was about to lose it; his mind was beginning to disintegrate. He loved his job so much and always loved helping people but his duties were starting to drain him emotionally and physically. He always went back home with a certain burden instead of a sense of fulfillment. His family could soon see the impact as he seemed so disconnected, he now goes about with a blank expression. He could not stand the sight of people in pain anymore.

Slowly, he began withdrawing himself from everyone and started having negative thoughts and emotions about life. He lost the desire for the activities he once found pleasure in. His sexual relationship with his wife was not spared, the bedroom soon became a cold room. These went on for a short while and after a few nights, his whole body felt heavy and he ached everywhere; before long, Bart was hospitalized.

It's very easy to fall into depression when you have to face emotionally draining situations every day of your life. While it is true that one of the duties of first responders is to offer encouragement and emotional assistance to people who are victims of disasters and all kinds of attacks, for the fact that they are dealing with such people and situations, it is very easy for them to fall into depression as well.

Let's say you must deal with rescuing people who are trapped under a collapsed building and you have to do this every day for one week, in a large-scaled event. You pull out dead and dismembered bodies, you watch as their family's members fall apart in inexpressible grief and you are there, watching it all. Doing this countless times can cause a build-up of emotions and if not addressed, you could go down the path of depression. We know that stress is cumulative and may not readily manifest itself in acute symptoms.

You don't have to be directly involved in an accident, incident or a disaster. We are all susceptible to stimuli that may affect or impact us all at various levels or degrees. Feelings are contagious and just being in the midst of depressive situations can influence you over time. The truth is that you may not even notice this in you until it becomes so deep-seated in your mind. The signs of depression can be subtle but there are noticeable signs that can help you detect depression quickly. In this book, my goal is to help members who are exposed to these types of incidents and stresses. I want to give them and their support systems signs and symptoms of theses issues. This is in order for us to quickly identify these and underlying issues of depression and stress; more importantly to break up this pernicious cycle and get them the help they need.

Be careful not to confuse this with having a bad day or "the blues."

Depression arises when these bad feelings and negative emotions remain for a long time and begin to affect your entire life.

Depression has the ability to alter every aspect of your life including your daily routines – affecting your eating, sleeping and even the way you think about life.

Here are a few signs of depression…

1. A feeling of extreme helplessness and hopelessness

This is a feeling that you can never move past your current level or when you feel that you are powerless to change bad situations. You feel that the circumstances of your life are beyond your control and you feel so sad about it.

2. You lose interest in things you once loved

You no longer find happiness in your hobbies, your family, your friends. You seemed drained at all time and lack the energy to do those things you once loved.

3. You experience a change in your eating habits

Once you notice you are gaining or losing weight drastically, this can be an early sign of depression.

4. Your sleeping habit also changes

You might find it difficult to fall asleep or you might be sleeping more than usual.

5. Sudden mood swings

You become easily angered. You discover that you cannot tolerate little things anymore. You also notice you are happy one moment and the next moment you seem lost.

6. Feeling drained and worn out

You discover that you cannot perform certain little daily activities as easily as before. Your body feels so heavy and you lack the motivation to do anything.

7. Feelings of discontent and emptiness

You feel completely worthless and discontented. You just don't seem to get anything right. This feeling overpowers you especially in situations where you find yourself you were you are not able to save someone and you end up feeling like a failure.

8. Addiction

You have an unstoppable urge for consuming alcohol, prescription drugs or other harmful substances. This may be an early sign of depression especially if you didn't engage in such previously.

9. Shortened attention span

You find that you lose concentration easily and find it difficult to focus on something for a long while.

These are just some early signs that something in you has changed. It may be your body's response to coping with all you have been through but depression, not treated becomes harmful in the long run.

There are several forms of depression and they are identifiable by their symptoms.

Major Depression: This kind of depression is a fairly common and according to the National Institute of Mental Health, about 16.2 million adults have experienced at least one major depressive episode. As with all forms of depressions, it does not solely rely on what's happening around you as those who are rich and famous, those who have loving families also suffer from major depression.

If it is not treated on time, it can last a lifetime. Some of the symptoms of major depression are difficulty sleeping, gloom, fatigue, excessive eating or a loss of appetite, lack of concentration, feelings of worthlessness, constant worry and thoughts of death and suicide.

Atypical Disorder: This is a form of depression that temporarily goes away in response to positive situations. Though it is very rare, it should not be regarded as less important as other forms of depressions. A lot of people become happier when they experience something positive like a visit from a longtime friend or time spent with loved ones but as soon as they leave, they sink back into depression. Some specific symptoms of this kind of depression are considerable weight gain, you begin to have more appetite than usual, you sleep too much, have strange sensations in your arms and legs and you become touchy and very vulnerable and sensitive to criticism.

Dysthymia: Also known as persistent depression, it is a form of depression that can last for as long as two years or more. The symptoms are not as severe as the others but as with every form of depression, it can affect your entire life and your relationships.

Some of the symptoms include the feeling of inadequacy, feeling of hopelessness, difficulty in concentration, social withdrawal, inability to feel or express joy.

Manic Depression: This is also known as Bipolar disorder. It is a constant state of alternating episodes of happiness and depression.

The symptoms of manic depression are similar to major depression but to be diagnosed with this Bipolar disorder, you must have experienced a considerable episode of mania – high energy, racing thoughts and speech, feeling euphoric, increased confidence and self-esteem.

Depressive psychosis: This is a form of depression where those affected lose touch with reality. They see, hear, and smell things that aren't there. Some patients claim to speak to people who aren't there. Some of the symptoms include lack of awareness and coordination, confusion, fear, and rage.

There are other forms of depression not mentioned in this book but the ones I mentioned are the most common forms of depression that fire fighters and first responders are prone to. A lot of people in this line of work are afraid to open up because they might feel that people will look down on them or it might make them look weak. This is our critical juncture. You need to let go of this mentality. There is absolutely nothing wrong with opening up to people who can help you. You might feel that it is up to you to save everyone (The Superman complex). Yes, it's true that we all look up to you as the hero in times of danger and you are doing a marvelous job but I gotta ask, who looks out for you?

This is a major "blind spot" for us and can mean the difference between danger or safety, safety or survival and, yes, even, life or death.

The people that you love and have relationship with you often may not have an idea of what you are really facing on the inside. You need to say something; you need to get help.

If you continue to keep these things to yourself and isolate yourself, it might transition into a disorder which will be a lot harder to cure. The sad issue is that we isolate ourselves, out of fear of being exposed. Yet, all of this is happening at a critical time when we need to connect to others.

Talking has a way of relieving the emotional and psychological build up. There is something about the way we are 'wired' as human beings that allows us to de-escalate stress and break up depressive cycles. Talk to that colleague of yours who is understanding and will not condemn you or talk to your spouse or significant other. If you don't want the people close to you to find out, then you can go to a confidential support agency, psychologist or therapist.

He, she or they will help you walk through the various emotions that you are experiencing and they can proffer solutions that will help you. At the very least, they provide you with alternative thoughts or provide accountability for your mental well-being.

Once you start experiencing these symptoms, do not wait until it gets worse. Seek help as fast as possible. Fortunately, there are various organizations that offer help specifically to firefighters, EMTs, medical personnel and police officers.

They are specially established to help first responders through what they go through which is caused as a direct impact of the nature of their jobs.

Dealing with depression

A lot of people have a negative attitude about depression but admitting you need help is the first and most important step of recovery. Depression like any other injury is not really self-inflicted but not seeking help is. No one may know exactly what you put up with at work, no one may really understand the burdens too heavy for your heart to bear –

- everyone, in one way or the other has gone through a depressing episode, what makes others depressed is how they handled it. I believe, with the right guidance and help, you can come out of that place of darkness, that place of void.

In my own experience, there have been times when recovery from traumatic stress was processed in a routine and 'matter of fact' manner. There have been other times that I still find challenges. What I know is that there are times when we cannot manage it on our own. Here are a few ways to help you combat depression...

1. *Take a step and reach out to people*

One of the persistent symptoms of depression is social withdrawal. On one end, you may feel that you don't need help. You can handle anything. On the other hand, you may feel ashamed of yourself or see yourself as weak or that you are a burden to your family, but this is not true.

You have to realize that your family and friends love you so much and they care about you. They will be devasted should you leave them. The pain, anguish and unanswered questions that you may leave in your wake only spawns a new cycle of pain and inflicts the same injury on others.

You have no idea how valuable you are, not just to your family but to your organization, your community and society. You have to commit yourself to keep reaching out.

Isolation is dangerous for you. When you stay on your own, you will seek destructive coping mechanisms. You will to dull the pin and nullify your emotions through self-medication.

Your thinking may even begin to wander to thoughts of drugs and suicide. Being around the people that care about you will really help you to manage depression. Confide in someone who you know understands you and will never condemn you.

They don't always have to proffer solutions, they just have to listen sincerely without condemning you, criticizing you or being judgmental.

Sometimes, what you need is a touch, a hug, a pat on the back, few words of encouragement. Have face to face discussions with the person you are confiding in. Seeing the faces of the people that you love can go a long way to lifting your mood and making you happy. At the very least, it will begin to balance out those negative feelings and impulses. Make time for social activities no matter how hard it is for you. Push yourself to attend social gatherings and resist the urge to stay away from people.

You could also get a pet; studies have shown that animal lovers are generally happier people. It will help you to take the focus off yourself and make you feel like you are needed. You could also join a support group, as seeing people that face what you are facing will help you to get rid of the notion that you are alone.

It will also help you give encouragement to other people as you now have the opportunity to share your own experiences.

2. Do activities that you enjoy

It is true that you may not find pleasure in some activities but you just have to push yourself.

Your feelings cannot be trusted at all because they are so volatile. Do you know you can trick your brain into feeling right?

When you engage in pleasurable activities, positive feelings will surely follow. Play video games, build a pet cage, learn a new language – you may not feel any change in your emotions immediately but give yourself time, you notice you've been revitalized and you're happier than you used to be.

3. Take care of your health

Depression has a way of affecting your mind and your body as well. Taking good care of your health in itself can tackle depression. Don't trivialize this aspect of your life. Do you know that the food you eat directly affects your feelings? Do you know that constant consumption of some substances like alcohol, nicotine, and caffeine can lead to depression?

It's true that sometimes you barely have time to eat your meals because of the unpredictability and stressfulness of your job, whenever you can, invest in supplements and health packs with protein, healthy carbs and fats, fruits, vegetables, the B vitamins, and omega 3 fatty acids.

4. Move your body

Exercise can fight every trace of depression in your life. It also helps to relieve the physical pain that comes with depression. Taking a 30-minute walk or jogging can help to keep you happy for up to two hours. Start small but make sure that you move your body every day. You will see how fast your fatigue disappears when you persevere. Find good exercise routines that have continuous rhythms like walking, dancing swimming. Just anything that will require you to move your hands and legs.

Be focused on how you feel when you exercise and pay attention to your body movements. If possible you can get an exercise partner. It can be a friend or a family member or join a gym.

5. Deal ruthlessly with negative thinking

This is the major battle that you have to face with depression. You have to be conscious of what goes on in your mind at all times. The negative thoughts you might be having are not the depression itself; they are only symptoms of depression. Depression usually starts with a negative experience. This experience creates negative thoughts and negative thoughts produce negative emotions. That is why you are prone to depression.

Your job requires that you face dangerous situations and heartbreaking events all the time. A lot of people are unable to bounce back after encountering just one traumatic event. What about you that is constantly in the midst of it all?

You go to work every day with the knowledge that you are putting your life in danger and this is something you have been doing consecutively for years. Your perceptions about life are very vulnerable to change and as time goes on, optimism is replaced by pessimism and negativity. Many first responders who work in the Emergency Medical Services begin to see mood changes after the same repetitive types of calls or resuscitating the same types of victims over, and over and over again. It will take some time to break free from the negative mindsets that have gained footholds in your mind. You have to start by challenging these mindsets and gradually replacing them with a new positive belief system.

The first thing is to identify these negative emotions.

Once you have done that, it's time to sit down with your mind and begin to challenge these thoughts and feelings one by one. Ask yourself how these mindsets have not helped you become a better person. Ask yourself how harboring these mentalities have not helped you in your work as well. You have to come to terms with the fact that you are emotionally vulnerable because of the kind of job you have and it's alright to feel the pain of other people.

It's alright to be human and vulnerable. Once we face this realization, we can begin to protect ourselves better. We will put on all of the personal protective equipment required to do our jobs in hostile and dangerous environments.

We will take the time to assess every tactical situation and strategy. We will "psyche" ourselves up to muster through trying situations. We will pair up and team up for our workplace challenges.

Yet, we will not hesitate once to take steps to protect our mind, our psyche or our mental health and wellbeing.

Our thoughts are more like you are a hero and everyone is looking up to you for help and encouragement. If you are not strong enough, how will you be able to help them?

The job of firefighters and first responders requires that you have to sustain a level of emotional and psychological strength – you have to be constantly fortifying your mind at all times. You have to protect your mind. Train yourself to be in control of your thoughts. Put a mental armor around your mind so that you will not be so easily affected by the traumatic incidents you have to handle. "Put on the whole Armor."

Strengthen your emotions as well so that you will have the fortitude to help the people that need you.

CHAPTER 2

War against Stress

Stress is usually associated with a feeling of being under severe pressure and is a big part of the downsides of this job. All jobs and careers have their own variations of stress but the peculiarity of your job is such that it has the capacity to pull you down if it is not managed properly.

You may always feel threatened and under pressure at all times. Your body releases the hormones: adrenaline, noradrenaline, and cortisol to help you handle difficult situations.

These hormones are not supposed to remain in your bloodstream but only to serve us when we need them. However, when we are constantly in difficult situations, these hormones stay in your body and this leads to stress and chemical changes in your body's other systems.

Stress that is not properly taken care of can lead to Secondary Traumatic Stress and Post Traumatic Stress Disorder.

Symptoms of stress

- You are constantly on edge and easily startled all the time. You find yourself constantly on your guard at all times.
- An abnormal sense of fear and trepidation, a residual thought that something bad will happen.
- Repetitive of nightmares.
- Racing and abnormal heartbeats.
- You experience tiredness, fatigue, aches, and pains all over your body.

There are several ways that you can avoid the effect of chronic stress…

▪ Work in groups

When next you go on rescue assignments, do it with a partner. This sounds simple enough however many people work together and do not feel as if they are part of the team.

Many times, connection is more important than what is being communicated.

When you go through challenging or difficult situations with someone who shares your concerns, both of you develop a bond and can share each other's concerns and problems.

▪ Take a break when you can

As noble as your job is and as indispensable as you are to society, the stresses and the emotional drain of your work can take its toll and weigh you down if you do not learn how to take some rest. You need to take care of yourself and recharge your emotional and psychological batteries, especially after a traumatic situation.

▪ Get yourself a hobby

Doing the things that you love will help you relieve a lot of stress. Fun activities are excellent ways to take out the stress from your life. Make sure that the activities you choose to indulge in during your recreation should not be work-related. Your purpose for doing this is to relax and take your mind off your work for some time.

▪ Exercise your body

Your body is constantly at work whenever you are called to respond to any situation. If your body is not in good shape, you will not be able to perform to the best of your ability and this will add to your feelings of helplessness. You will end up increasing your cortisol levels. Find a good routine that works for you and exercise regularly.

It has been discovered that exercise can increase the production of endorphins which has the capacity to improve your mood and lessen signs of irritability. This will give you a good boost and revitalize you when next you go for a rescue mission.

▪ Meditate

Meditation is a great way to relieve stress before and after a hard day's work. Meditation helps you to see the beauty of nature and opens your eyes to the many beautiful things that you have. It takes your eyes off the bleakness of the situations that you have to encounter every day. Meditation can also reduce pain and help you to unclutter your mind. Combine this with some simple yoga activities and deep breathing and see yourself transform remarkably. Practicing deep breathing is a great way to alleviate stress and has a very soothing and calming effect on your mind and body.

▪ Write in a journal

Writing down your feelings in a book can get you in tune with what is going on in your life. You will get to understand the way your mind works and it will also help you clarify your emotions. This is especially vital when you have just been through a painful and emotionally draining event.

If you do not want to open up to anyone about what you feel, you can use a journal. Writing is just like talking to yourself. There is also no danger of people discriminating you at all. In this case, you are like your own therapist.

▪ Talk to a counselor

There are certain things that you just cannot keep to yourself. When you keep traumatic experiences inside you for a long time, they can eat so deep into your mind and become disorders or even lead to a complete disorientation of your mind.

Talking to a professional about what you are going through can go a long way to help you cope with whatever emotional turmoil you are going through.

▪ Be part of a group

Being part of a group will help you connect to those who are in the same shoes as you and learn from them as well.

Generally, you have to deal with stress during and after a traumatic situation. When you are on duty you experience a range of emotions such as anxiety, severe emotional pain, nausea, failure to sustain a considerable amount of concentration, numbness, fear, sorrow and all kinds of negative thoughts. Become more mindful of these feelings.

After the incident, you are also not spared of stressful feelings. You may find it difficult to sleep and you may also begin to have nightmares as well. Stress, if left untreated, can spill over to your family and cause you to have conflicts with your loved ones.

CHAPTER 3

When the Pain is Unbearable

Peter was at his breaking point but nobody had any idea of it. He just could not stand it anymore. For the last two weeks, he had been involved in pulling out dead bodies from beneath a collapsed building, pulled out charred remains of a family of four that had burned in a car accident and two days ago, had been on the scene of a crime where a 5-year-old girl had been brutally raped and dismembered by a serial killer who was still on the loose. Add to all of this, Peter is a military veteran with multiple tours overseas as a Combat Medic.

With each rescue mission, he had to attend to, the pain had increased tremendously. He could no longer stand the sight of the tragedies anymore. He had not been able to save any of them. He began to feel that his life was worthless and there was no point to it. What was the need of having a duty to save lives when he could not save any of those people? He could not take it anymore. He would end it now and for all. He waited for the night to become dark enough and hurried to the bridge. As he stood at the top of the bridge overlooking the river, he decided that he had no reason to keep on living. Life was so full of tragedy and he could not stand the pain anymore. Closing his eyes, Peter jumped off the bridge and fell to his death. Peter left a caring family and workmates who are left with unresolved questions, pain anguish and guilt.

Somewhere on the other side of town, Jude had purchased a whole packet of sleeping pills.

He was determined to end his miserable existence that day. He was a firefighter and due in hours ago, had been notified of a car that was stuck on a train track. All endeavors to stop the train had proved futile and Jude kept hoping that they would get there on time. He and his crew had sped there as fast as they could, and his heart was pounding all the while. Unfortunately, just a few minutes to getting there, they watched in horror as the train ran over the car. It was too late.

Jude was numb at first. When they got to the car they saw the mangled bodies of a man, woman, a 2 or 3-year-old boy and 6 month-old-baby. It was late at night at exactly 2 am and it was on the outskirts of the city. Jude could not come to terms with what had happened. He could not believe what he had seen. He felt like a total failure.

While the rest of his colleagues were tearfully pulling out the bodies, Jude felt numb. He went on with his job like a robot. His colleagues could not understand him. They had no idea of the years of trauma and depression that had been building up inside him. They had always thought he was just an unemotional guy but they had no idea that the last bastion had been shattered. Jude was going to kill himself. After the paramedics and EMTs had arrived and they had succeeded in clearing the scene, Jude hurriedly stole away to a drug store and purchased the sleeping pills. He went to an abandoned construction site and completely fell apart. He cried his eyes out but still, the pain refused to go away. He popped several amounts of the sleeping pills into his mouth and a few minutes later, died with tears in his eyes.

The statistics of first responders especially firefighters that commit suicide are staggering. Statistics show that the number of first responders that commit suicide annually is twice the number of ordinary citizens. We are beginning to see patterns in the behavior and demographics. This may be surprising but it's very true.

You see, the nature of your job is such that you are constantly in the midst of negative situations.

It's not easy to pull out bodies from car accidents or collapsed buildings, it's not easy to help victims of rape and other types of catastrophes, it's not easy to comfort a 3-year-old who just lost her entire family in an armed robbery attack. It takes so much emotional strength to these things every day of the week.

You constantly have to respond to terrible situations every day of your work week.

It's not surprising at all that some police officers or fire fighters give in to suicidal thoughts. When everything you see is negative, it can affect your mind in a terrible way. Suicidal thoughts are directly related to untreated depression and stress disorders. If you ever notice these signs, then you need to seek help immediately.

- Feelings of utter hopelessness
- Unexplainable and excruciating emotional pain
- Indulging in addictive habits
- Isolating yourself from your friends and family and everyone
- Beginning to think or talk about killing yourself
- Constantly criticizing and beating yourself down
- Beginning to think that you are a burden to everyone around you and that they will be better off if you are gone
- Drastic changes in your personality
- Having thoughts about death consistently
- Purchasing and looking for items and substances that you can use to take your life.

When you see these signs in your life or in a colleague of yours, that is not the time to keep quiet or believe that everything is going to be alright. You have to seek help fast! The reason why suicide is so prevalent and close relatives or friends of people who committed suicide had no idea of it was because the person kept these things to himself or herself.

This is the most dangerous thing to do. Reaching out can stop suicide right in its tracks and help you get your life back. You are far too valuable to the world to take your own life no matter what you have to face.

Think about all the people who have directly gone through the emotional trauma that you have witnessed. Somehow, they kept on surviving and found the strength to move on. You are not alone.

You cannot give in to suicide because all you see is the bleakness of life. You are far more than that. You put your hand up and swore an oath to protect life. That oath includes your life, too!

Your friends need you; your family needs you and our society cannot do without your bravery and selflessness.

Never entertaining thoughts of hopelessness. You have to realize that although helping people as part of your job, sometimes you cannot save everyone.

34

You do not have the power to stop the bad things that happen every day. You have to be strong not just for yourself but for the people who look up to you. There are very few people who can do what you do, there are very few people who are as selfless as you are, so do not for any reason give up on yourself or think that you are worthless. You are so much more than you realize.

Even in the face of all the bad things that happen, there is still so much good and beauty in the world and you are one of the reasons why people find the strength to move on. You are one of the reasons why there is still good in society. You give countless people hope that there is a lot more to life so never see yourself as worthless. Your very presence makes a difference in the lives of others.

Having a burden to save people while simultaneously putting yourself in danger all the time is a feat that is almost impossible for the average person but you are doing it.

You have to appreciate the facts of your work and sustain the emotional strength to be there for the victims that you have to rescue.

In times like this, our families and friends are wonderful sources of emotional support for us. Do not isolate yourself from people especially those that love you. Share your pains with them or an understanding friend. It can go a long way to help you see things clearly.

My friends, you must speak up and speak out. It sounds simple, I know. You have to share the weight of your situation with someone else. It's tough to admit that you have these problems and a lot of firefighters have expressed concern about the discrimination that happens in the workplace when someone is found to be suffering from one emotional and psychological issue or the other.

Even so, there are numerous agencies that have been set apart to advocate for first responders. Like I said before, if you do not want to confide in your boss or colleague, you can always talk to your family or see a therapist.

The important thing is that you do not, in any way, hold it in. You just have to talk to someone about it. It can help.

When you open up about your challenges, it encourages your colleagues to do the same as well and you will get to see that you are not alone in what you are facing. You will also end up saving as many people as you can from eventually committing the act. When they see how much happier you are, they will realize the need to come out and seek help. This singular act can encourage firefighters, EMTs, police officers, and military personnel all over the world and you can make a positive impact in the lives of your fellow colleagues.

CHAPTER 4

Dealing with Grief and Loss

You were in your office one day chatting happily with your colleagues in the short time you guys had to rest a little and talk when you suddenly received an order to rush to a fire incident. You all scattered in different directions as you prepared yourselves and rushed to the scene of the fire. It was an apartment building and then while you were trying your best to put out the fire and then just when you and your colleagues have successfully put out the fire and seen to every other thing that you have to take care of, all of a sudden, a gunman from nowhere shoots five of your colleagues down and escapes immediately in a bike.

It all happened so fast that you don't even know how to comprehend what just happened to you. After the incident, you discover that you and one other person survived the attack. What do you do in the face of such a devastating event? How do you deal with the painful feeling of loss and grief? You can't believe that the same guys that you were happily talking with are gone just like that.

Unfortunately, a lot of first responders die in the line of duty. It is so painful beyond words to lose your colleagues and friends in a twinkle of an eye. So many questions keep running through your mind and it seems like you can never come to terms with reality. You even end up feeling guilty that you survived.

Many people grieve differently but we all experience the five stages of grief. Unfortunately, some people never reach the last stage.

We do not necessarily have to experience them in any particular order but it is important to know what happens in each stage so that you can know where you are with your feelings and also monitor your grieving.

Here are the five stages of grief...

1. Denial: The first reaction to grief and loss is often denial. You refuse to believe the reality the person is gone. You deliberately numb your emotions and feelings. You begin to see life as worthless and void of meaning. At this point, denial actually serves to buffer the shock and reduce the unimaginable pain that you feel. Sometimes you may even want to isolate yourself from everyone else.

No matter how much a person wants to remain in this stage, reality does eventually set in.

2. Anger: This is when the dust settles and you begin to see things more clearly. The pain you have been trying to avoid and deny comes back in full force. You start to become angry and your hurting mind starts to look for someone to blame. You may blame your friends family, yourself and even the person or people that you have lost. You feel that they have caused you pain. Deep down inside, you know that there is absolutely no reason for you to blame them and this makes you even more angry with yourself.

3. *Bargaining:* This is when you begin to feel guilty. You feel that there must be something that could have been done or something that you could have done to save them. Myriads of "if" questions begin to flood your mind; "If only we had put out the fire sooner," "if only I had seen the gunman on time and stopped him, "if only the police were there with us," "if only we had stayed inside the building a little while longer," if....if.....if...if. You ask yourself these questions because you are so burdened by guilt. Sometimes you may even wish that there was a way you can postpone the event that has happened or move back the hands of time. All this is done in a bid to get rid of the helplessness of your situation.

4. *Depression:* This kind of depression comes in two forms, the first is that you can feel extent sadness and regret as you come to terms with the practicalities of what has happened. You begin to see how much you may have neglected those who need you. Sometimes, the solution to this is some encouragement and kind words or spending time with your loved ones. The second kind is when you withdraw from people. You begin to prepare your heart to let go of the one(s) you have lost. Sometimes, the only thing you need is a hug and a kind presence.

5. Acceptance: It is quite sad to say that not everyone gets to this point in their grieving. This is the place where you find peace. You have come to accept the reality of what has happened and you know that they are not coming back. You feel calm and you may also want to withdraw a little.

Not everyone is strong enough to get to this point though and you will need all the help you can get. It's true that you know the risks of your job and you know that you will always be in danger whenever you are on duty but an event like this can shatter your emotions especially because it was unexpected.

Dealing with loss and grief is something that a lot of people find very hard to do and it's even harder for people in this particular line of work but here are some tips that can help you deal with loss and grief when an unexpected tragedy like this occurs while on duty.

Don't hide it, talk about it: If you want to heal faster, you have to talk to someone about what you have experienced.

Talking helps to clear your feelings up and help you to see situations more clearly. In this case, the best thing to do is to see a therapist. You can always trust a therapist to keep whatever information you tell him or her in confidence.

Many times people who want to support you may feel awkward and/or inadequate. They try to fill the silent void with helpful banter. Please don't judge them too harshly. Their attempts are their way of showing you that they care for you and about this situation. They just haven't found the proper words or timing.

Look for balance: After witnessing a disaster, it can color how you begin to see life. You might begin to think in a pessimistic way about life in general and it can blind you from seeing the real picture. Keep on reminding yourself of the good things that you have, the good things that have happened to you and the good that you can do. Keep in mind that your colleagues died being heroes and that is who you are as well.

Take a break from the news for a while: It is good to be aware of what is going on around you and it is definitely essential concerning the nature of your job but constantly listening to catastrophic events happening all over the world will not help in your healing process. It does not hurt to turn off the television for a while. Hearing bad news all the time will increase your cortisol levels and will not help you to cope with your feelings of grief. It will only serve to make things worse. Stay away from the TV for a while and stop replaying news videos on your portable devices, at least until you are completely recovered.

Don't ignore your feelings: Part of the healing process is acknowledging and accepting your feelings. Don't ignore your pain. Deal with it and you become better with time.

Look after yourself: This is the time that you need to take time out and properly take care of yourself.

Invest in healthy eating and plenty of rest. Please don't give in to drugs or alcohol in the hopes that they will make the pain go away. They will only make things worse and leave you feeling miserable. They are also harmful to your mental and physical health as well.

Help others and be productive: Helping other people has a way of making you happier. Look for ways to help people no matter how little you can. This will enable you to see how much good there is still to be done and will help you take your mind off pessimistic and negative thoughts and mindsets.

Be patient: Don't be in a hurry to heal. Grieving takes a reasonable amount of time and different people grieve in different ways and for different periods of time.

Do activities that will make you happy and lift your spirits while allowing your heart and mind to heal properly.

Enjoy the people and things you love and when your mind begins to drift towards that traumatic incident, train yourself to shift focus to positive things instead. It may be necessary for you to get rid of anything that may remind you of that incident and this is another reason why you have to take a break from the TV for some time. Surround yourself with things that make you happy. Enjoy the company of your loved ones and get some much-needed rest. Whatever you do, avoid negative activities and learn to enjoy life.

Coping with loss is a difficult and personal experience but you can do it. Just allow the healing process to continue uninterrupted. With time, the pain will fade away.

Allow yourself to feel and do not try to resist the pain. It will come and go naturally.

CHAPTER 5

Oblivion vs Reality

James' colleagues had always wondered how he could maintain a clear-headed focus on the job. While the rest of them had tried to keep themselves from falling apart,

James seemed to be immune to the stress and emotional drain of what they had to go through every day.

Sometimes they wouldn't even have a chance to sleep for five seconds for days on end and at other times when they had managed to secure some time to relax, an emergency would come up and they would have to rush to the rescue. In all this, it seemed that James possessed a superhuman mind and heart. They didn't notice the needle marks on his arms or the slight powdery leftovers on his nose. They did not notice that he took a considerably long time in the bathroom.

They did not notice the shaking episodes or the way his eyes and hands twitched. All they saw was a man that was always full of energy. One fateful day, the truth came out to the open. As soon as they finished their breakfast, they were about to leave for a rescue mission when they discovered that James was nowhere to be found. They searched for him all around the fire station but couldn't find him.

They decided to check the bathroom and saw James lying down on the floor and shaking uncontrollably in his hands were packets of white powdery substances and a syringe. He was foaming in the mouth as well.

They rushed him to the hospital but it was too late. James was dead. The autopsy report came out: **Cause of Death: Drug Overdose.**

It's not very surprising for first responders to take to drugs and alcohol for emotional support whenever the stresses of their jobs take their toll on them.

Drugs seem to offer a means of escape from the painful stresses of life that they face every day. One pill turns to two and then increases until the person gets sucked into the whirlpool of drug addiction.

Whether you are a first responder or your loved one is, you can help your colleagues or loved one to get out of this destructive habit because the truth is that while it seems to offer temporary solutions, it can permanently destroy a persons life. These are some signs to look out for if you have a loved one in this line of work.

- You start to notice that he or she has burned fingers or lips
- You spot needle marks on the person's arms
- The person's speech may be slurred and/or incoherent
- The person has trouble maintaining eye contact
- His or her pupils are dilated or constricted irrespective of light
- The person begins to have tremors
- He or she has bouts of shaking or convulsions.
- His or her eyelids and hands begin to twitch uncontrollably
- You notice that he or she is so hyperactive
- He or she may begin to show signs of lethargy

- The person seems to have impaired coordination
- The person either speaks too fast or too slow
- He or she begins to have extreme mood swings
- He or she may become fearful or anxious for no reason and may experience panic attacks
- He or she becomes easily angered and defiant
- His or her tolerance level drops to a significant low and they become very irritable.

As you have read in the preceding section, their moods and appearance can run from one extreme to another and may just be subtle changes. Take notice.

Defeating the Monster of Addiction

The first step to winning the war over addiction is to decide to change. The decision has to come from you. If you are forced or coaxed into it, you won't be able to carry through to the end. You have to want to change. Drug abuse alters your brain chemistry in bizarre ways and although you get a temporary escape from your problems, it just makes everything worse in the long run. Using drugs will not take away your problems. As painful as that is, it is the truth. You have to confront them head-on. That is what makes you strong. When you do decide to change and STOP this bad habit, there are some things you have to keep in mind.

You have to take note of the number of drugs you use and the type. You have to also keep track of when and how often you use the drugs.

Write down all the benefits you stand to gain by stopping the habit.

This will help you stay motivated throughout your process of treatment and recovery.

Think about the important things in your life: Consider your family and friends, the people that need you, the many people that you can help save their lives, think about how invaluable you are to your community and society.

Look deep inside yourself: Is there anything that might stop you from quitting? Is there any reason whatsoever why you do not want to quit drugs? Be honest with yourself and write these things down. On the journey to recovery, there are some necessary steps you need to take to ensure that you reach your goal. Keep reminding yourself of the reasons why you decided to change in the first place. Quitting drugs is a difficult process that requires great discipline and willpower. There will be times when you will feel like giving up but you have to encourage yourself. Find a sponsor or a reliable contact who will hold you accountable to your stated goals and commitments. Set goals and targets for yourself. Give yourself landmarks and limits. Pay attention to your surroundings and get rid of anything that is likely to trigger an urge for drugs at work and in your home.

Seek support: Tell your friends and family about your decision and ask them to help you.

Your family can be a great source of support in times like this. Now that you have made your decision, there are several treatments that you can choose from although the kind of drug you are addicted to will determine the treatment that you need.

Detoxification: This is usually the first step and it involves cleaning your entire system to get rid of any drugs that are present in your bloodstream. It also helps you to deal with withdrawal symptoms.

Behavioral Counselling: This involves a series of therapy sessions that serve to help unearth the root causes of your addiction and also repair your relationships.

Medication: Medication can give you relief from withdrawal symptoms, keep relapse at bay and also treat any other underlying problem you may have such as anxiety and depression.

Long term follow-up: Having a system of follow up can really help you to avoid relapse and keep you sober. You may need to attend some support groups on a consistent basis to help monitor your recovery.

Types of Treatment Programs

1. Residential Treatment

In this method, you will be required to leave work and reside in a treatment facility. You will receive a series of intensive treatments and it may last for a few days or months depending on the severity of the addiction.

2. Partial hospitalization

If you would like to remain at home and still continue with your job, you can go for this treatment method. The only thing is that you will have to spend 7 - 8 hours at the facility or hospital and then return home in the night time. You can opt for night shifts so that it won't stop you from going to work.

3. Outpatient Treatment

This treatment affords you the opportunity to be treated close to your workplace. The major target of this treatment is to prevent any form of relapse.

4. Sober living communities

If you feel that you need more time and that you are not ready to resume work or that staying at home may trigger a relapse, there are facilities where you can live with other addicts who are also on the road to recovery. This is very similar to the first kind of treatment and you get good quality care and support without any form of discrimination. This is also a great option if you feel like you have nowhere else to go.

You have to find a treatment method that works well for you. Whichever treatment you choose, always try as much as you can to make sure you attend meetings regularly. Don't keep silent to what is happening with you. You cannot face this problem alone and you need the support of the people who love you.

Do not give up on yourself as there are millions of people going through the same thing as well.

Though you may not know this, there may be some of your colleagues who are also passing through the same struggle but they might be hiding it. Don't go to drugs as a means of relieving stress, **IT DOES NOT HELP AT ALL!**

There are so many healthy ways of relieving stress so creating a routine of recreation that is suitable for you.

CHAPTER 6

Sometimes Superheroes Need Help Too!

All superheroes have to take a break from saving lives to remember that they also need saving as well. Superman takes off his suit and enjoys being Clark Kent, Batman leaves his cave for some time so that Bruce Wayne (Author's note: I'm Batman) can participate in normal activities. You can be so caught up in saving the day that you end up neglecting yourself. Taking care of yourself will also help you become more effective at work. There are some tips that have already been mentioned above but I will group them all under self-care. These are the things that you can do to take the stress off your job.

- **Reduce your working hours:** Your working hours should not be more than 12-hour shifts. This will give you some time to relax and get your mind back in order.

- **Work with a partner**: Working with a colleague will help you reduce the emotional pressure that comes with the job.

- **Journaling**: Writing in a journal is a great way to get in tune with your emotions and can help you uncluttered your mind.

- **Don't neglect your friends and family**: Being in the company of the people you love will help you take your mind of the burdens of your work.

- **Practice Deep Breathing**: Take some time out to practice deep breathing and meditation. This is a great calming technique that is even recommended by doctors. It helps to soothe your heart and expel excess build-up of adrenaline in your system.

- **Set boundaries**: Be careful not to work beyond your capacity. If you know that you are certainly not physically and emotionally fit for an assignment, so not be afraid to decline. You will do yourself and your organization a lot of good by working when you are effective.

- **Stay away from alcohol:** Alcohol does no good! It will only cause harm to your mental health. Indulging in drinking will also make you become vulnerable to other harmful behaviors and addiction may also follow.

- **Have some time to yourself:** Take a walk in the park or in the woods and just enjoy the beauty of nature. You will be pleasantly surprised to see how much clearer your perspective will become. You will begin to see life from a whole new dimension and you will find yourself being grateful for the opportunities that you have to save lives and be a source of hope to thousands of people.

- **Stop complaining:** Complaining to people will not solve your problems at all. There is a difference between talking about what you are facing and complaining about it. Complaining makes you seem ungrateful and selfish. You might even come off to some people as rude. When you talk to people about your issues, especially if you desire to let your organization know what has been going on with you, do it without a sense of entitlement and resist blaming your colleagues or your boss.

- Move over to the positive side

Don't dwell only on the negative sides to your job. Be grateful for the opportunity to help people and provide emotional support to people who need it. You don't have to wear a mask and a cape before you become a hero. Recognize your value to society and never forget it.

Before going on a rescue assignment, there are some certain things you have to do before, during and after that will help you become more efficient.

Before a rescue mission

1. Make sure that you have enough training to do what you are supposed to do. You should also have enough knowledge and skill about how to handle difficult and emotional situations and prevent them from affecting you negatively.

2. You also have to know your duties and responsibilities at the scene of the mission as well.

3. Do some self-examination. Check to see if you are under any form of mental stress. If you are, it may not

be wise for you to go for any assignment until you are in a proper emotional state. Any imbalance in your emotions will disrupt your work and also that of your colleagues as well.

4. Check if you're physically fit. You should not be on duty if you are sick or have any illness of any kind. You will put yourself and your team in danger. You have to be physically fit to help people.

5. Maintain contact with your colleagues at all times.

During a rescue mission

1. Maintain your focus and try as much as you can to concentrate on what you are doing. Whatever you do, eliminate any form of distractions.

2. Pay attention to what you are feeling at every point in time. Do not allow your emotions to get out of control. Be conscious of your surroundings at all times as well.

3. If you begin to notice that your feelings and reactions are getting out of control, do not hesitate to ask for help from your colleagues. You cannot continue in such a state and you may fall apart.

After the rescue mission

1. Find a way to express your feelings. Don't keep it in. It is important for you to do this after every job that you finish so that you don't fall into depression and anxiety. A major cause of depression among first responders is that they do not let out their feelings until it keeps piling up and leads to depression. You can do this by writing or even talking about your feelings out loud. Do this when you are alone in a quiet place.

2. Seek assistance if you feel that you cannot withstand your emotions on your own.

3. **Isolation is dangerous.** This is not the time to stay away from friends and family. They are your greatest sources of support, comfort, and encouragement.

4. Go back to your daily routines. Having a sense of sameness can really help you achieve balance in your life.

5. Stay active, the nature of your job is such that you are always on the move at all times so it is important that you are constantly physically and mentally active at all times. Avoid any activity that will keep you in a place for a long period of time.

Don't stop being a Hero

Every job has it's own good days and bad days but that is quite an understatement for first responders. Not everybody can take on the responsibilities that you have to face every day. You save people from danger while putting yourself in danger. Not to mention the severe emotional and psychological stress you in encounter in every rescue mission.

Sometimes, we even take you for granted and fail to appreciate the sacrifices that you make every day on behalf of everyone. No one knows the secret pains and injuries that go on inside you with each assignment. You are not alone in your pain. There are thousands of your fellow colleagues sharing the same pain.

It always takes the best and strongest of us to do the things that we cannot do. You are part of the select few who have decided to sacrifice your lives for the greater good. Like all heroes, this duty comes with its fair share of pain and tragedy. Watching others suffer while being unable to help is a feeling that very few people can handle.

I just want to let you know that you are indispensable. This nation would not be able to survive without your sacrifices. Even if you do not receive an award or a public acknowledgment, think about the many lives that you have saved, think about the families that are indebted to you. That in itself is a reward.

You have the right to enjoy the beauty and good things in life. Do not allow depression, stress, anxiety, and grief to paralyze you.

Few people can boast of having a job that helps to save lives. People can trust you with their lives. Rejoice in the active part you play in giving hope to thousands of people. You stand as a symbol of what is best in our society.

Maximize this opportunity you have to touch as many lives as you can. The most rewarding job in this world is one that allows you the chance to touch people's lives and leave an impact that will last forever. There is nothing as fulfilling as someone walking up to you and saying "I made it because of you," "Thank you for changing my life," "You gave me strength when I needed it and I did not lose hope because of you."

Don't dwell on the situations that you had no power to change. Sometimes, it takes a lot more strength to accept the fact that there are some things we cannot change. Some situations will be beyond your control and you do not have to beat yourself up over it. You do so much good every day and that is more than enough to bring you fulfillment. So get up on your feet and keep on being a source of hope and light to our world.

We need you. I need you. I need you to fight for your life!

Suicide Prevention Help:

Public: https://suicidepreventionlifeline.org/1-800-273-8255

Fire: https://www.firstrespondercenter.org/

Police: https://www.badgeoflife.org/

Veterans: https://www.veteranscrisisline.net/

ABOUT JOHN ALSTON

John Alston is a 34-year veteran of Emergency Management. He is a John Maxwell Certified Speaker, Executive Coach, Trainer and Behavioral Analyst. He came to the **John Maxwell Team** with over 25 years of experience as a trainer. As a First Responder to the World Trade Center, on September 11, 2001, John witnessed leadership and courage on a grand scale which impacted his life forever.

For the last two years, John has served as the Fire Chief of the New Haven Fire Department. John is a retired member of the Jersey City Fire Department, with over 31 years there. As a former Master Instructor for the International Association of Fire Fighters, John trained hundreds of firefighters, fire officers and first responders around the nation. He is a certified Instructor-Trainer through the National Fire Academy and the American Red Cross. He is the former Operations Director and Chair of Curriculum for the Carl Holmes

Executive Development Institute where he trained and coached hundreds of Emergency Management Officers to become Executive Officers. John has been blessed to travel and train all over the world.

John is, currently, the Executive Director of the Fire Officer Trust where he coaches First Responders, Law Enforcement Officers and Emergency Management Leaders in their command roles and responsibilities during large-scale emergencies.

John is a frequent keynote speaker and panelist on a variety of topics, from Leadership and Emergency Management to Response to the Opioid Crisis.

In the arena of leadership, Alston sets himself apart, by focusing on the people, before the problem. He works from connections, in communications. Alston's passion lies in the development, support and encouragement of First Responders.

OTHER WORKS

- *The Seven C's of Fire Officer Trust*
- *Handling Personnel Issues in the Workplace*
- *The Secret Sauce in Leadership*
- *Fireproof Leadership*

www.fireofficertrust.org

www.leadleaderlead.net

59883762R00043

Made in the USA
Middletown, DE
13 August 2019